SONGBOOK

perrysongs

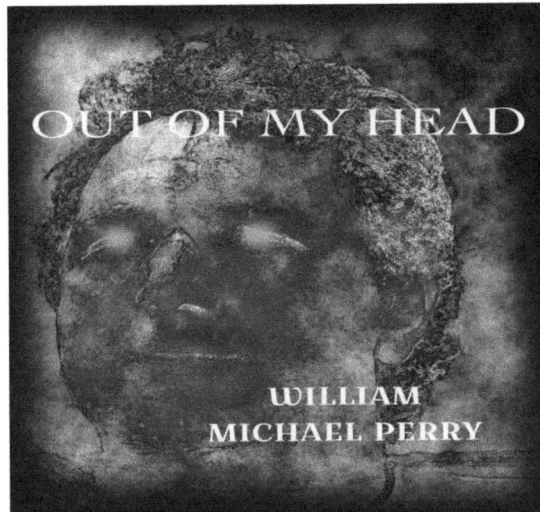

Perrysongs Music Publishing ltd

Auckland NZ

First Published 2021

ISBN : 978-1-99-115751-5

PRINTED IN USA

Acknowledgements:

Special thanks to Nick Jones @ Nick Jones Music for his expert assistance in scoring this material.

"Out Of My Head" by William Michael Perry is available from major download stores worldwide
Catalogue # PMP017

All Talk

♩ = 78

Words & Music by B. Perry

I'll wait out-side   you can de-liv-er the bad   news,   just tell it like it is, and I have

ever-y faith_   and con-fi-dence in your a-bil-i-ty_   to shine.

I'll   wait   in_____ back   you can put forward the mo - tion   we must

play   to   our   strengths,   I   will   be   right   here_   though I   won't

_ a-ppear my   yel - low streak will   see   to   that.   Be-cause I'm all

_ talk   and no ac - tion   it's   a   cha - rac-ter flaw,   that I   poss- ess

_____   you know I'm all__ talk   and   no   ac tion,_   I guess.

2

27 G^maj7   D^maj7

29 G^maj7   D^maj7

31 Em^7   F#m^7   G^maj7   D^maj7

I'll wait out - side   you can de-liv-er the bad news,   we must

34 B^7   Em^7   A^7

play to our strenghts___   I have ever - y faith___ and

36 F#m^7   Bm^7   Em^7   Ebm^7(b5)   D^9(sus4)

con - fi-dence in your a - bil - i - ty___ to shine.   Be-cause I'm all

39 Em^7   D^maj7   Em^7

___ talk and no ac - tion   it's a cha - rac-ter flaw, that I poss ess

42 D^maj7   D^9(sus4)   Em^7

_____ you know I'm all___ talk and no ac tion,___ I guess.

45 G^maj7   D^maj7

47 G^maj7   D^maj7

3
49 Bm7 D7 Em7 Bm7 D9(sus4)
(instrumental)
54 Gmaj7 Gmaj7 Dmaj7 Gmaj7 Dmaj7
Be-cause I'm all
59 Em7 Dmaj7 Em7
talk and no ac - tion it's a cha - rac-ter flaw, that I poss ess
62 Dmaj7 D9(sus4) Em7
you know I'm all talk and no ac tion, I guess.
65 Gmaj7 Dmaj7
67 Gmaj7 Dmaj7
69 Em7 F#m7 Gmaj7 Dmaj7
I'll wait in back you can put for-ward the mo - tion we must
72 B7 Em7 A7
play to our strengths, I will be right here though I won't
74 F#m7 Bm7 Em7 Ebm7(b5) D9(sus4)
a-ppear my yel - low streak will see to that. Be-cause I'm all

talk and no ac - tion it's a cha - rac-ter flaw, that I poss ess

_____ you know I'm all__ talk and no ac tion,_ I guess.

Fantasy Women

♩.=116

Words & Music by B. Perry

Em⁷   D⁶(add9)   Em⁷   D⁶(add9)   Em⁷   D⁶(add9)   C   D   Em⁷

9 Em⁷   D⁶(add9)   Em⁷   D⁶(add9)

Got a love-ly litt-le la-dy called Claire,   Beau-ti-ful brown eyes and blo-nde hair,

13 Em⁷   D⁶(add9)   C   D   Em⁷

un for-tu-nate-ly she is fic-tion-al,   and I need to get fric-tion-al   with a girl.

17 Em⁷   D⁶(add9)   Em⁷

Know a-noth-er litt-le hon-ey called Sa-rah,   she loves me dear and who can blame

20 D⁶(add9)   Em⁷   D⁶(add9)

her,   Oh the baw-dy times we   share,   are on-ly spoiled

23 C   D   Em⁷   Am⁷   Bm⁷

by my re-al-i-ty__ check.   Fan-tas-y wo-men   al-ways will-ing   oh the strokes

27 Am⁷   Em⁷   Am⁷

that they get up to in my head,   fan-ta-sy wo-men   fine and dan-

30 Bm⁷   E°⁷   B⁷

dy   but a litt-le of the real thing,   would sure ly come in han- dy_____

2

33 Em⁷ D⁶⁽ᵃᵈᵈ⁹⁾ Em⁷ D⁶⁽ᵃᵈᵈ⁹⁾ Em⁷ D⁶⁽ᵃᵈᵈ⁹⁾ C D Em⁷

I know a gor

41 Em⁷   D⁶⁽ᵃᵈᵈ⁹⁾   Em⁷

geous ir-ish girl, name of Nua-la,   there's no - thing that you would-n't want to

44 D⁶⁽ᵃᵈᵈ⁹⁾   Em⁷

do with her,   I see her ever-y time I close my

46 D⁶⁽ᵃᵈᵈ⁹⁾   C   D   Em⁷

eyes,_ A luxur-y vi-sion in my mind_____ Fan-tas-y wo-

49 Am⁷   Bm⁷   Am⁷

men   al-ways will-ing   oh the strokes that they get up to in my

52 Em⁷   Am⁷   Bm⁷

head, fan-ta-sy wo-men   fine and dan-dy   but a

55 E°⁷   B⁷

litt-le of the real thing,   would sure-ly come in han-dy_____

57 Em⁷ D⁶⁽ᵃᵈᵈ⁹⁾ Em⁷ D⁶⁽ᵃᵈᵈ⁹⁾ Em⁷ D⁶⁽ᵃᵈᵈ⁹⁾ C D Em⁷

65 Em⁷ ... D⁶⁽ᵃᵈᵈ⁹⁾ ... Em⁷

Of course there's Em-ma, Sue and Jane,___ three in-di-vid-uals none

68 D⁶⁽ᵃᵈᵈ⁹⁾ ... Em⁷ ... D⁶⁽ᵃᵈᵈ⁹⁾

the same, but when they ga-ther in my head, there's ve-ry litt-le

71 C ... D ... Em⁷ ... Am⁷ ... Bm⁷

room left there in the bed, Fan-tas-y wo-men al-ways will-ing oh the strokes

75 Am⁷ ... Em⁷ ... Am⁷

that they get up to in my head, fan-ta-sy wo-men fine and dan-

78 Bm⁷ ... E°⁷ ... B⁷

dy but a litt-le of the real thing, would sure ly come in han-dy_____

81 Em⁷ D⁶⁽ᵃᵈᵈ⁹⁾ Em⁷ D⁶⁽ᵃᵈᵈ⁹⁾ Em⁷ D⁶⁽ᵃᵈᵈ⁹⁾ C D Em⁷ *(2x)*

..hot, like a ja-le-pe - no, She's hot, like a ja-le pe - no, She's..

89 Am⁷ ... Bm⁷ ... Am⁷ ... Em⁷

(improvise solo)

93 Am⁷ ... Bm⁷ ... E°⁷ ... B⁷

First Congregational Church

Words & Music by B. Perry

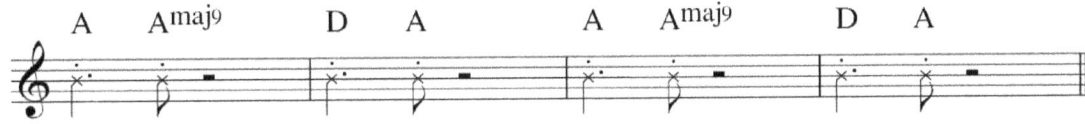

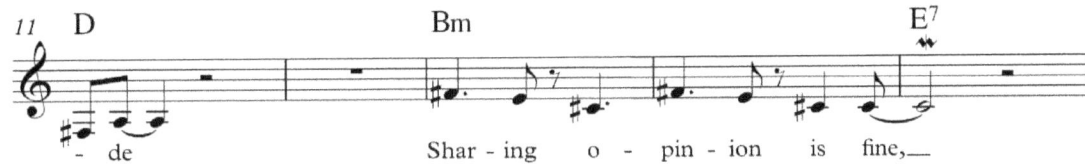

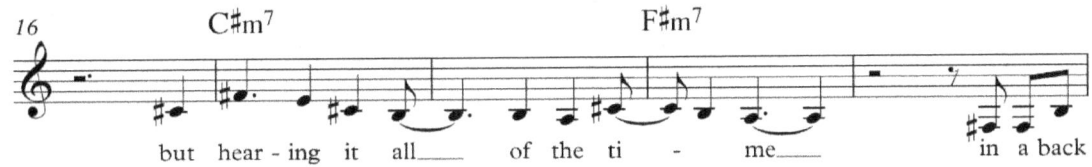

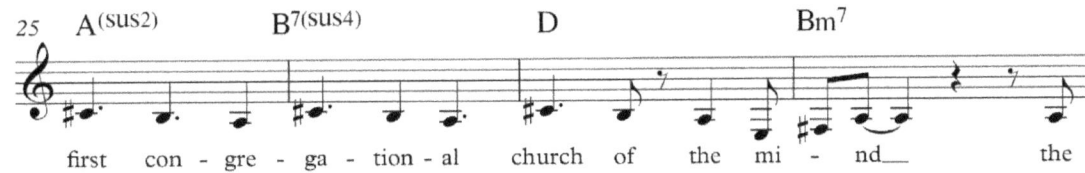

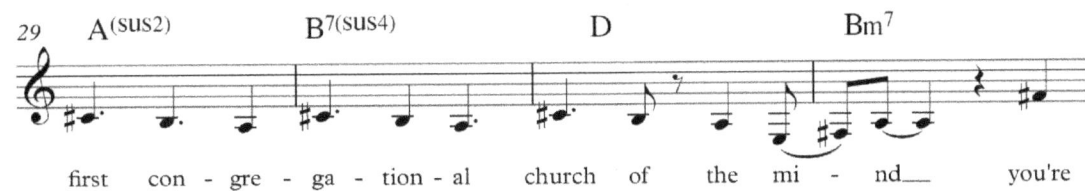

♩=150

Learn to de - ci - pher the code,_ don't let your val - ues e - ro - de

Shar - ing o - pin - ion is fine,_ but hear - ing it all_ of the ti - me_ in a back room, in a va - cuum in_ the first con - gre - ga - tion - al church of the mi - nd_ the first con - gre - ga - tion - al church of the mi - nd_ you're leav - ing your heart_ and your I - Q be - hi - nd, in the

2
37 A(sus2) B7(sus4) D Bm7
first con - gre - ga - tion - al chuch of the mi - nd__ all
41 A Amaj9 D A A Amaj9 D A
rise.
45 A(sus2) Em7
Air-waves will carr - y the news_ po - li - ti - cal shades, tints and
51 D Bm E7
hues. W - ear - ing you down by__ de- grees,_
56 C♯m7 F♯m7
bring - ing you down_ to your knee - s. sub- scribe
61 Bm E7
__ now and don't doubt, don't doubt the
65 A(sus2) B7(sus4) D Bm7
first con - gre - ga - tion - al church of the mi - nd__ the
69 A(sus2) B7(sus4) D Bm7
first con - gre - ga - tion - al church of the mi - nd__ you're

3

73 A(sus2) B7(sus4) D Bm7 A(sus2)

leav-ing your heart_ and your I____ Q be-hind_ in the first con-gre-

78 B7(sus4) D Bm7 A Amaj9 D A

ga - tion-al church of the mi - nd_ all rise. And you're

83 C#m7 A(sus2) C#m7

leav-ing it there_ for good it won't come back

88 A(sus2) F#m7 ⌐3⌐

__ like it should, if you, o-pen u - p your hear

93 Bm7 Bm7

- t then you'll feel be - tter right

96 E7

__ from the start.

99 A F#m D Bm

103 A F#m D Bm (repeat 4x)

The

4

A(sus2)　　　　　　B7(sus4)　　　　D　　　　　　Bm7

first con - gre - ga - tion - al church of the mi - nd___ the

A(sus2)　　　　　　B7(sus4)　　　　D　　　　　　Bm7

first con - gre - ga - tion - al church of the mi - nd,___ you're

A(sus2)　　　　　　B7(sus4)　　　　D　　　　　　Bm7

leav - ing your heart,_ and your I____ Q be - hi - nd in the

A(sus2)　　　B7(sus4)　　　　D　　　　Bm7 C#m D E A(sus2)

first con - gre - ga - tion - al church - of the mi - nd, all rise.

rit.

13

Five Stars

Words & Music by B. Perry

♩ = 140

Lyrics:

She got eyes ___ that smoul der bright-ly like em-bers in a fi-re, dia -monds on her fing-er-s a litt-le wig-gle in her walk she looks ___ good e-nough to eat but too dan-ger-ous to talk to___ she got five ___ stars.

She looks sa-ssy on___ the cat walk where she's full of fe-line grace has a fun-ny litt-le half frown that she wears_ u-pon her face___ though her

2

37 Am⁷ D⁹⁽ˢᵘˢ⁴⁾

ears   drip sil - ver_ she's as cul - tured as a pearl_ she got five

41 Gmaj7 Cmaj7

_   stars   not one,

45 Fmaj7   Em⁷   Am⁷   D⁹⁽ˢᵘˢ⁴⁾

two,   three,   four_____ but five

49 Gmaj7 Cmaj7 1.

_   stars.

53 Cmaj7 2. Gmaj7 Cmaj7

Instrumental

58 Gmaj7 Cmaj7 Am⁷

64 D⁹⁽ˢᵘˢ⁴⁾ Gmaj7 Cmaj7

69 Gmaj7 Cmaj7

3
She has a

74 Gmaj7   Cmaj7

pho - to - gen - ic nose   that she flares— when she's an-noyed   but that

78 Gmaj7   Cmaj7

ve-ry rare-ly hap - pens 'cos she's friends with all— the boys— she makes love on

82 Am7   D9(sus4)   tr

ly with the cam - era   and she'll— ne-ver lose her poise—   she got five

86 Gmaj7   Cmaj7   Fmaj7   Em7

— stars,   not one,   two,

92 Am7   D9(sus4)   tr Gmaj7   Cmaj7

three,   four———— but five— stars.   s

97   Gmaj7   Cmaj7

                                          3
she gives in-

102 Gmaj7   Cmaj7

- ti-mate ex - clu - sives to gloss - y mag-a- zines— she's seen in all

106 Gmaj7   Cmaj7   *3*

— the hot-test night - clubs in one thou-sand doll-ar jeans— she would

4

love to make a mo - vie she says life ain't what it seems. she got five

stars, Not one, two,

three, four_____ but five___ stars

not one, two,

three, four_____ but five___ stars.

Her Life's A Play

♩=198

Words & Music by B. Perry

Old the - a - tri - cal pos - ters_ co - ver walls

_ that are_ ol - der, there she sits_ thumb-ing

pro-grammes to bits_ can- dles_ lit_ .

Scans the pa - ges for her name, fad-ing rem-nants of

her_ name, kept a- live_ though her still ac - tive

mind is on re - wind._ Her life's a play

_____ all_ the world is her_ stage her life's a play

_____ a lead-ing role to be play - ed_

53 Cmaj7 F♯7 Bmaj7 Em7
On an ov - er-stuffed so - fa too much gin in her
59 Bm7 F♯m7 Fmaj7 Em7 3
so - da wear-ing lace though she
64 Em7 3 A7 Dmaj7 Dmaj7
still paints her face there's no grace.
71 Cmaj7 F♯7 Bmaj7 Em7
There's no man to ro - mance her, though she once loved an
77 Bm7 F♯m7 Fmaj7 Em7 3
act - or, she gave up him now she rue - full - y
83 A7 Dmaj7 Dmaj7
grins at her sins Her life's a play
89 Bm7 F♯m7
all the world is her stage her life's a play
97 Bm7 F♯m7 F♯m7
a lead-ing role to be play - ed

3

105 Cmaj7 F#7 Bmaj7 Em7
(instrumental solo)

111 Bm7 F#m7 Fmaj7 Em7

117 A7 Dmaj7

123 Bm7 F#m7

129 Bm7

134 F#m7

139 Cmaj7 F#7 Bmaj7 Em7
when she tour-ed the coun-try__ all her friends thought her__

145 Bm7 F#m7 Fmaj7 Em7
luck - y__ with a frown__ as the cur-tain comes

151 A7 Dmaj7 Dmaj7
down she won-ders when__ they all are now.__

4

157 Cmaj7 F♯7 Bmaj7 Em7
Dreams of mak-ing a come back once ag- ain meet her
Bm7
163 F♯m7 Fmaj7 Em7
pub - lic, she can-not face time
168 A7 Dmaj7 Dmaj7
has quick-ened it's pace she's lost the ra - ce. Her life's a play
175 Bm7 F♯m7
all the world is her stage her life's a play
183 Bm7 F♯m7
a lead-ing role to be play - ed her
191 Bm7 Bm7
life's a play, her life's a play, her
195 F♯m7 F♯m7
repeat and fade to end.
life's a play, oh, her

Hooray For The Girl

Words & Music by B. Perry

Am7   F#m7(b5)   Bm7   E9(sus4)

Instrumental

Am7   F#m7(b5)   Bm7   E9(sus4)

Spring is in the air I feel it in my bone,

Am7   F#m7(b5)   Bm7   E9(sus4)

sus-pec-ted ti-dal wave of lust might hit my home.

Dm7   E9(sus4)   Dm7   E9(sus4)   Fmaj7

Knock me for a loop turn my brain to soup I al-ways

Em7   Dm7   G7

lose my nerve_____ when I see her curve I go Hoo-

Cmaj7 Dm7   Em7   Dm7   Cmaj7 Dm7   Em7   Dm7

ray___ hoo - - ray___ hoo

Cmaj7 Dm7   Em7   Dm7   Bm7   E9(sus4)

ray___ for the girl.

Am7   F#m7(b5)   Bm7   E9(sus4)

Instrumental

2
33 Am7 F#m7(b5) Bm7 E9(sus4)
Flash-y teeth and eyes_ make me all_ a flutt - er_
3
37 Am7 F#m7(b5) Bm7 E9(sus4)
lips that smile_ at me they turn my legs_ to butt - er_
41 Dm7 E9(sus4) Dm7 E9(sus4)
must be nat - ures way_ or God had a good day
45 Fmaj7 Em7 Dm7 G7
_ with that ex - tra rib_ it's a hell_ of a trick_ so hoo
49 Cmaj7 Dm7 Em7 Dm7 Cmaj7 Dm7 Em7 Dm7
- - ray_ hoo - - ray_ hoo
53 Cmaj7 Dm7 Em7 Dm7 Bm7 E9(sus4)
ray_ for the girl.
57 Am7 F#m7(b5) Bm7 E9(sus4) Dm7 E9(sus4)
Improvise
repeat, to play 4x
63 Dm7 E9(sus4) Fmaj7 Em7 Dm7 G7

69 Cmaj7 Dm7 Em7 Dm7 Cmaj7 Dm7 Em7 Dm7

Hoo - ray___ hoo - - ray___ hoo

73 Cmaj7 Dm7 Em7 Dm7 Bm7 E9(sus4)

ray___ for the girl.

77 Am7 F#m7(b5) Bm7 E9(sus4)

Instrumental

81 Am7 F#m7(b5) Bm7 E9(sus4)

Spring is in the air I feel it in my bone,___

85 Am7 F#m7(b5) Bm7 E9(sus4)

sus-pec - ted ti - dal wave of lust might hit my home.___

89 Dm7 E9(sus4) Dm7 E9(sus4)

Knock me for a loop turn my brain to soup

93 Fmaj7 Em7 Dm7 G7

I al-ways lose my nerve___ when I see her curve I go Hoo

97 Cmaj7 Dm7 Em7 Dm7 Cmaj7 Dm7 Em7 Dm7

ray___ hoo - - ray___ hoo

101 Cmaj7 Dm7 Em7 Dm7 Bm7 E9(sus4) Am7

ray___ for the girl. hoo -

If The Tiger Disappears

♩ = 108

M. Griffiths & B. Perry

"If the tiger disappears why then, should we cry it's..

..not as if, we're going to miss all those tiger pies, and sar-

-torially speaking, stripes are really, quite passe and

orange, as a colour, it just doesn't suit me anyway, as a rug,

they are offensive they're all teeth, and shoe worn skin now they

tell me, that the bones, are crushed, and are used in chinese medicine,

2

43 Bm⁹ ... Bm⁶

47 Bm⁷ ... B♭m⁷ ... D⁷/A ... D⁷⁽ˢᵘˢ⁴⁾ Bm/A

instrumental melody

53 A♭⁽ᵃᵈᵈ⁹ˢᵘˢ⁴⁾ ... A♭ ... D♭⁶/A♭ Fm⁷/A♭ E♭m⁷/A♭

57 Em⁷ ... Bm

"so if the tiger disappears ... *it won't cause us any pain*

61 Em⁷ ... Bm ... A

it will however be, of course to our, eternal, shame.

66 Em⁷ ... Bm ... A A ... G F♯m⁷ Em⁷

75 ... Bm ... A A ... G F♯m⁷

82 Em ... Em ... Em⁹

89 ... Em ... Em ... Em⁷⁽ᵃᵈᵈ⁴⁾

Joe's The Man

♩ = 122

Words and Music by B. Perry

Gm⁷

Joe's

Cm⁷ · Gm⁷ Cm⁷ Cm⁷ · Ab⁷
__the man, with a smile_ and a glare,_ that might keep__you in line, from his hat

Dm⁷ · Gm⁷ · Cm⁷ · Ab⁷
- to his croc - o - dile shoes, Joe's_the man I would Choo - se__See him

Cm⁷ · Gm⁷ · Cm⁷ · Ab⁷
ou - t girl_ in to - w on the town,_ in his G.__ T. O. he's a m-

Dm⁷ · Gm⁷ · Cm⁷ · Ab⁷
an, who likes to get things done, Joe's_ the man, num - ber o - ne

Cm⁷ · Gm⁷ · Cm⁷ · Ab⁷
improvise solo

Dm⁷ · Gm⁷ · Cm⁷ · Ab⁷ **D.S al Coda**
(repeat 4x then take the D.S)

CODA
Gm⁷/C · Gm⁷

Living It Up

Words & Music by B. Perry

2

37 Em⁷

bass line　　　*sim.*

41 Em⁷

(add chords)　　　　　　　　　　　　　　*2nd time →* No

45 Em⁷

lunch at two___ se - cret ren dez - vous,___ no

49 Em⁷

Cham - pagne or___ oys - ter bars I'm___

53 Em⁷

home by___ eight___ at the ph - ones___ I'll wait___

57 Em⁷

hang-ing with___ su-per stars.___ It may

61 Am⁷　　　　　Bm⁷　　　　　　　Em⁷　　　　A⁷

seem so un - so-phis-to - cat-ed___ just

65 Am⁷　　　　　Bm⁷　　　　　　B⁷

head___ phones and a groove___ And I'll be

69 Em⁷ ... A⁷ ... A⁷ ... Em⁷ Dmaj⁷ Cmaj⁷ Bm⁷
liv-ing it up_ liv-ing-it up_ liv-ing-it up_ all night

73 Em⁷ ... A⁷ ... A⁷ ... Em⁷ Dmaj⁷ Cmaj⁷ Bm⁷
liv-ing it up_ liv-ing it up_ liv-ing it up_ all night.

77 A⁹ ... Em⁷ ... Play 3x
(instrumental)

81 A⁹ ... B⁷

84 ... Em⁷
bass line ... sim.

89 Em⁷
(add chords) ... 2nd time → No

93 Em⁷
tea at three, at the Ri - tz_ for me_ no

97 Em⁷
Cham- pagne or_ su - shi_ bars_ I'm at ho

4
101 Em7
- me, by__ eight__ at the pho - nes_ I'll wait__
105 Em7
hang-ing with__ su-per stars______ It may
109 Am7 Bm7 Em7 A7
se - em so un - so-phis-to - ca- ted__ it's just
113 Am7 Bm7 B7
head phones loud__ and a groove.__ And I'll be
117 Em7 A7 A7 Em7 Dmaj7 Cmaj7 Bm7
liv-ing it up_ liv-ing it up_ liv-ing it up__ all night,
121 Em7 A7 A7 Em7 Dmaj7 Cmaj7 Bm7
liv-ing it up_ liv-ing it up liv-ing it up__ all night
125 Em7 Dmaj7 Cmaj7 Bm7
liv-ing it up_ liv-ing it up__ liv-ing it u - p all night
129 Em7 A7
liv - ing it up___ liv - ing it up___
131 A7 Em7 Dmaj7 Cmaj7 Bm7 Em7
liv-ing it up__ all night

More Headlines

Words & Music by
B. Perry & A. Curtis

♩ = 90

Head-lines say the Queen has sneezed at the__club, some rich fool has hurt his hand in a__

__ fall I__ would like to know the ans - wer__

is the coun-try rea-lly bo-thered at all__ uh - huh,

Soc-cer yob es capes the law with a fine, it makes the front page of the tab-loids eve

- ry time I__ would like to know the ans - wer

have they found a cure for can - cer uh - huh,

guitar solo

harmonica solo

2

28 A ... F#m ... A ... F#m ... A ... F#m

Head-lines say the but-cher boy got__ the knack of get-ting ve-ry rich a voi-di-ng tax

31 A ... F#m ... Bm⁷ ... C#m

__ and I__would like some of that ac-tion but the tax-man got my ass in trac-tion

34 Bm⁷ ... A ... F#m ... A ... F#m ... A ... F#m

oh-oh uh- huh__ Head-lines say there's al-ways room at the

38 A ... F#m ... A ... F#m ... A ... F#m

__ top and free en - ter-prise is a closed shop and all__

41 Bm⁷ ... C#m ... Bm⁷

__those head-lines I have read put puzz-led lines on my fore head__ oh__

44 A ... F#m ... A ... F#m ... A ... F#m

will keep read-ing the head - lines__

47 A ... F#m ... A ... F#m ... A ... F#m

I'll keep read-ing the head - lines I'll keep rea-ding the

50 A ... F#m ... A ... F#m ... A ... F#m ... A

will keep read-ing the *fade out to end*

Mr. No Show

♩ = 120

Words & Music by B. Perry

Mis-ter no show you know him well but his in- tent you
can-not tell__ his__ smi-ling face is one of two__ don't turn your
back I'm__ warn - ing__ you__
Mis-ter no show you love the bars where you can pose as
one you are- n't__ the mas-que- rade is ov-er soon be-cause your
friends are on - to__ you__
Mis-ter no show he'll tell you lies but with a twink-kle in his eyes
a pro-mise made_____ is soon for- got__ hol-low words,
sure e- nough__

2
30 Cmaj7 B9(sus4) Em7
Mis-ter no show how is your son? Oh come on now you
33 B7(sus4) E♭maj7 Dm7
know the o - ne__ he is the gift____ you tossed a-way when you
36 G7 Cmaj7
3
aban-doned his____ on his bir - th - day
39 Cmaj7 B9(sus4) Em7 B7(sus4)
Mis-ter no show is there no clue what fills the space in - side of yo-u__
43 E♭maj7 Dm7
your con-science clear____ you al-ways say__ I don't know how
45 G7 Cmaj7
__ it stays that way___
48 B(sus4) B7 Em7 A(sus4) A7
Mis-ter no show he'll tell you lies_ but with a twink - le
51 Dmaj7 E♭maj7
in his eyes__ a pro - mise made_____ is
53 C9(sus4) Fmaj7 Bm7(♭5) B♭maj7 D9(sus4)
soon for got holl-ow words, sure enough__

3

59 C Am⁷ F G

percussion *brass section*

65 C Am⁷ C /B /A /B C C /B

69 Cmaj7 B⁹(sus4) Em⁷ B⁷(sus4)

percussion only Mis ter_ mis ter_

77 E♭maj7 Dm⁷ G⁷ Cmaj7

mis- ter_ no show

82 B(sus4) B⁷ Em⁷ A(sus4) A⁷ Dmaj7

Mis-ter no show he'll tell you lies but with a twin kle in his eyes

86 E♭maj7 C⁹(sus4) Fmaj7 Bm⁷(♭5)

a pro-mise made___ is soon for got_ holl-ow words sure e- nough

90 B♭maj7 D⁹(sus4)

percussion only

—

97 C C♯ D D♯ E F F♯ G C

single bass notes, no chords.

New York Ways

♩ = 98

Words & Music by B. Perry

Am⁷ Bm⁷ Dm⁷ Em⁷ Fmaj7 Dmaj9

(improvise)

5 Am⁷ / Bm⁷
See Che-vy's a-qua-pla-ning, the screech of tire on track

7 Dm⁷ / Em⁷ Fmaj7 Dmaj9
Ci-ca-das in the ma-ple will hum 'till night is black

9 Am⁷ / Bm⁷
I miss the mor-ning ba-gel fresh cof-fee in a cup

11 Dm⁷ / Em⁷ Fmaj7 Dmaj9
the bea-ches on___ the week-end send-ing blood pres-sure up

13 B⁷(♯9) E⁷(♯9) Am F♯m⁷(♭5)
I miss my New York days, my New York ways I miss 'em all

17 B⁷(♯9) E⁷(♯9) Am⁷
I miss my New York days,

20 Am⁷ / Bm⁷
The stea-my heat of sum-mer the clear and end-less sky

22 Dm⁷ / Em⁷ Fmaj7 Dmaj9
The ride to Be-ar Moun-tain, a chan-nel thir-teen drive

24 Am7
Bm7
Tac - ton - ic Park - way gil - ded, lu - min - ous in the fall
26 Dm7
Em7
Fmaj7
Dmaj9
No sleep with - out the A/ - C, my god I missed it all
28 B7(#9)
E7(#9)
Am
F#m7(b5)
I miss my New York days, my New York ways I miss 'em all
32 B7(#9)
E7(#9)
Am
I miss my New York days
35 Am7
Bm7
Dm7
Em7
Fmaj7 Dmaj9
39 B7(#9)
E7(#9)
Am
F#m7(b5)
B7(#9)
E7(#9)
Am
(Drum fill)
46 Am7
Bm7
Wor - king in Green - wich 'C T' high roll - ers eve - ry - where
48 Dm7
Em7
Fmaj7
Dmaj9
Armed cops on tra - ffic du - ty, no "ma'am you can't cross there".

50 Am7
Bm7
The A - & - P for shop-ping, Em - por - i - um if flush,
52 Dm7
Em7 Fmaj7 Dmaj9
Life in West-ches - ter coun - ty, I could not get e-nough
54 B7(♯9) E7(♯9) Am F♯m7(♭5)
I miss my New York days, my New York ways I miss 'em all
58 B7(♯9) E7(♯9) Am
I miss my New York days
solo pick-up
61 Am7 Bm7 Dm7 Em7 Fmaj7 Dmaj9
65 B7(♯9) E7(♯9) Am F♯m7(♭5)
69 B7(♯9) E7(♯9) Am7

Only For You

Words & Music by B. Perry

♩ = 172

brass

Bm⁷ B♭m⁷ Am⁷ Am⁷

My ba-by has eyes on-ly for you, *(trumpet)*

6 G   Em⁷

my ba-by has eyes on-ly for you____

10 Am⁷

I don't know what_ I'm go-ing to do____

14 G   Em⁷

my ba-by has eyes on-ly for you____   It's

18 Cm⁷   Cm⁷

all   o - ver now,

22 F⁹(sus4)   G

all____ o - ver town,   It's

2

She Had Everything

Words & Music by B. Perry

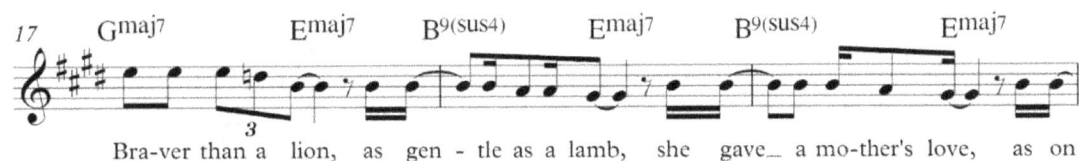

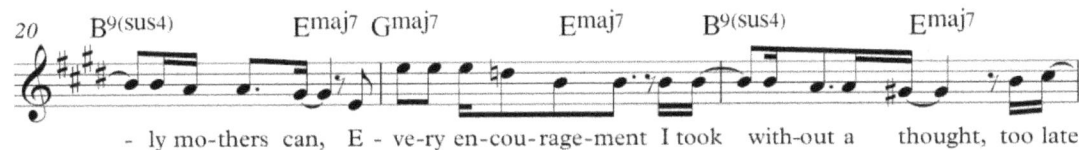

She had eve-ry thing she had the look, the grace, the style

bi-da-bi-dup-ba-ba__ She gave eve-ry thing, she

gave my life and then__ her time.

Bra-ver than a lion, as gen-tle as a lamb, she gave__ a mo-ther's love, as on

-ly mo-thers can, E-ve-ry en-cou-rage-ment I took with-out a thought, too late

__now for a-pol-o gies too late__ be-cause-she's gone, She had e-ve-ry thing

a pu-re soul, and heart__ and__ mind.

2
31 Emaj7 Cmaj7
She had eve - ry thing her- sac - ri - fice for
34 B9(sus4) Emaj7 Emaj7
me and__ mine, in all_
37 Gmaj7 Emaj7 B9(sus4) Emaj7 B9(sus4) Emaj7
__the years I loved her I nev-er un-der- stood ex- act - ly what she meant to me, or
40 B9(sus4) Emaj7 Gmaj7 Emaj7
what a good son does, for ten - der words are use - less when un - spo
42 B9(sus4) Emaj7 B9(sus4) Emaj7 B9(sus4)
- ken in your head the liv - ing years go rush-ing by and they_re- main un- said.
45 Emaj7 Cmaj7 B9(sus4) Emaj7
improvise solo
51 Emaj7 Cmaj7 B9(sus4) Emaj7
57 Gmaj7 Emaj7 B9(sus4) Emaj7
Thank you is a phrase that ne - ver says e - nough and so_
59 B9(sus4) Emaj7 B9(sus4) Emaj7
__ my heart will keep the se - cret of my__ un - spo-ken love,_

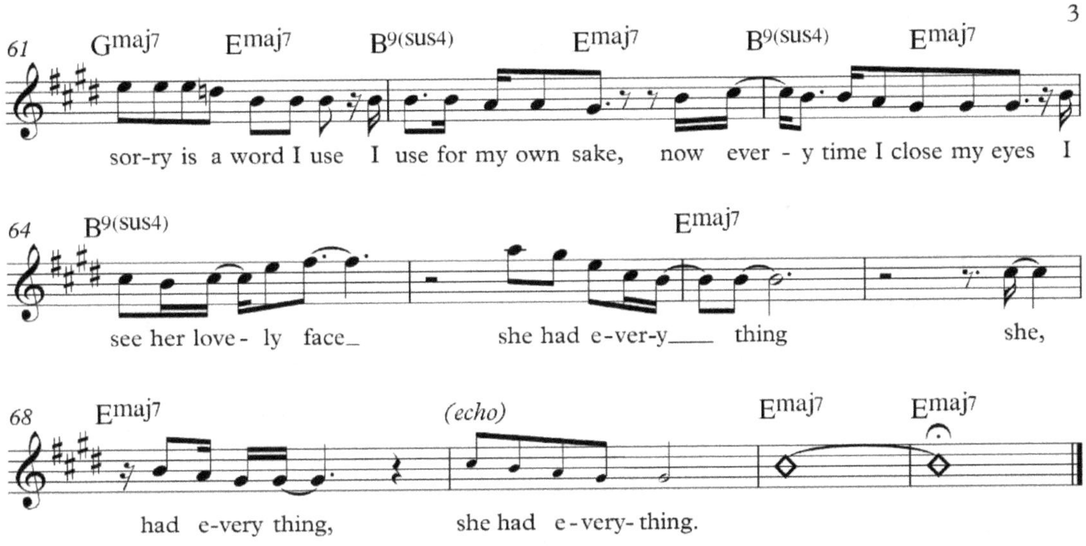
3
61
Gmaj7
Emaj7
B9(sus4)
Emaj7
B9(sus4)
Emaj7
sor-ry is a word I use I use for my own sake, now ever - y time I close my eyes I
64
B9(sus4)
Emaj7
see her love- ly face_ she had e-ver-y___ thing she,
68
Emaj7
(echo)
Emaj7
Emaj7
had e-very thing, she had e-very- thing.

Sweet Sweet Love

Words & Music by B. Perry

♩ = 100

Play Intro 3x (Brass 2nd & 3rd time only)

Brass — fp

5 Am7 — Dm7 — G9(sus4) — Am7 — Dm7 — G9(sus4)

"Sweet sweet sweet sweet love,"_ You're gon- na Feel__ it

9 Am7 — Dm7 — G9(sus4) — Am7 — Dm7 — G9(sus4) G7

"Sweet sweet sweet sweet love," You're gon na need it This e-

13 Am7 — Dm7 — G9(sus4) — Am7 — Dm7 — G9(sus4)

mo tion it will cause you pain you best a- void__ it but there

17 Am7 — Dm7 G9(sus4) — Am7 — Dm7 — G9(sus4) Dm7

rea-lly is no hi ding place you can't des-troy it em

21 Em7(add11) — Dm7 — Dm7

bra-cing it with o -pen arms you're at the mer - cy of it's charms

25 Am7 — Dm7 — G9(sus4) — Am7 — Dm7 — G9(sus4)

"Sweet sweet sweet sweet love," You're Gon na need it

2

29 Am¹¹   Dm⁷   G⁹sus⁴   Am¹¹   Dm⁷   G⁹sus⁴

Brass

fp   *fp*

33 Am⁷   Dm⁷   G⁹(sus4)   Am⁷   Dm⁷   G⁹(sus4)

If you want your life with out   com-pli-ca - tions

37 Am⁷   Dm⁷   G⁹(sus4)   Am⁷   Dm⁷   G⁹(sus4)   Dm⁷

Can cel your sub scrip-tion to   love's ob-li-ga - tions   They're

41 Em⁷(add11)

cree - ping   in   the   back   door   now   And you

43 Dm⁷   Dm⁷

must - n't   let   your   guard   go   down

45 Am⁷   Dm⁷   G⁹(sus4)   Am⁷   Dm⁷   G⁹(sus4)

"Sweet sweet sweet sweet love," You're gon-na feel   it

49 Am¹¹   Dm⁷   G⁹sus⁴   Am¹¹   Dm⁷   G⁹sus⁴

Brass

fp   *fp*

improvise solo

If you want your life with out   Comp-li-ca - tions

Can-cel your sub scrip-tion to   Love's ob-li-ga - tions   They're

cree - ping in the back   door   now   And you

83
Dm7
must - n't let your guard go down
Dm7
85
Am7
Dm7
G9(sus4)
Am7
Dm7
G9(sus4)
"Sweet sweet sweet sweet love," You're gon- na feel it
89
Am11
Dm7 G9sus4
Am11
1. 2. 3.
Dm7 G9sus4
4.
Dm7 G9sus4
Brass
fp
fp

The Money And The View

♩ = 80

Words & Music by B. Perry

Drums only

Instrumental

She sat

eat-ing mas-car-po - ne,_ sip-ping her la -tte while per

us-ing her co - py, of the New Yor-ker's page and their

month-ly re- view in-form-ed her_ a- new the

old-est things in green-wich were the mon-ey and the vi-ew,

Here's t - o the vie - w, the mo-ney an-d the view

He sat

2

33 Em7

slum-ped all a-lo-ne, at the end of the bar— in his

37 Em7

sa-ville row su-it, and his Ga-ber- dine scarf, his

41 Em7

glass raised a toast, to no one that— he kn-ew,

45 Em7

here's to the life-style, the mon-ey and the vi-ew,

49 Am7   Em7   C#m7(b5)   D9(sus4)

Here's t-o the vie-w, the mo-ney an-d the view

1.   2.
55 Em7   Em7   F#m7   Gmaj7   F#m7   Bm   A

59 Cmaj7   Cmaj7   Em7   Em7

improvise solo

63 Cmaj7   Cmaj7   B(sus4)   B7

They were

3

67 Em⁷

ma-de for each oth- er,   their cul-tures a-ligned   shared an

71 Em⁷

in-ter- est_ in art,   and   all things su- blime,   Though they

75 Em⁷

ne -ver would   meet,   it was just   some - thing that I kn- ew,

78 Em⁷

they be - liev - ed   in   the life - style

80 Em⁷

the mon-ey   and_   the vi- ew,

83 Am⁷   Em⁷

Here's   t - o the vie - w,   the

87 C#m⁷⁽♭5⁾   D⁹⁽sus4⁾   **1.**
                                        Em⁷

mo - ney   an - d the view___

2.
91 Em⁷   F#m⁷   Gmaj⁷   F#m⁷   B⁽sus4⁾ B⁷   A

fine

Other songbooks by the same author..........

Anthology (ISBN 978-0-473-53232-1)

 100 Songs (ISBN 978-0-359-30892-7)

Home County/Treading Water Songbook (ISBN - 978-1-991157-50-8)

P.S. -The Songs of William Michael Perry and Gary William Steaggles (ISBN 978-0-473-5627-2)

Out Of My Head Songbook (ISBN 978-1-991157-51-5)

The Bill Perry Songbook (Volume One) (ISBN 978-0-473-47060-9)

Unsung - The Instrumental Music Of William Michael Perry (ISBN 978-1-0670185-0-4)

www.ingramcontent.com/pod-product-compliance
Lightning Source LLC
Chambersburg PA
CBHW080524090426
42734CB00015B/3154